Focus on Marijuana

Focus on Marijuana
A Drug-Alert Book

Paula Klevan Zeller
Illustrated by David Neuhaus

TWENTY-FIRST CENTURY BOOKS
FREDERICK, MARYLAND

Published by
Twenty-First Century Books
38 South Market Street
Frederick, Maryland 21701

Text Copyright © 1990
Paula Klevan Zeller

Illustrations Copyright © 1990
David Neuhaus

Printed in the United States of America

10 9 8 7 6 5 4 3 2

Library of Congress Cataloging in Publication Data

Zeller, Paula Klevan
Focus on Marijuana
Illustrated by David Neuhaus

(A Drug-Alert Book)
Includes bibliographical references.
Summary: Describes the history, effects, social aspects,
and physical dangers of using marijuana.
1. Marijuana—Juvenile literatue.
2. Marijuana—United States—Juvenile literature.
[1. Marijuana. 2. Drug Abuse.] I. Neuhaus, David, ill.
II. Title. III. Series: The Drug-Alert Series.
HV5822.M2Z45   1990
362.29'5'0973—dc20   89-20430 CIP
ISBN 0-941477-97-5

Table of Contents

Introduction

"Baby Saved by Miracle Drug!" "Drug Bust at Local School!" Headlines like these are often side by side in your newspaper, or you may hear them on the evening news. This is confusing. If drugs save lives, why are people arrested for having and selling them?

The word "drug" is part of the confusion. It is a word with many meanings. The drug that saves a baby's life is also called a medicine. The illegal drugs found at the local school have many names—names like pot, speed, and crack. But one name for all of these illegal drugs is dope.

Some medicines you can buy at your local drugstore or grocery store, and there are other medicines only a doctor can get for you. But whether you buy them yourself or need a doctor to order them for you, medicines are made to get you healthy when you are sick.

Dope is not for sale in any store. You can't get it from a doctor. Dope is bought from someone called a "dealer" or a "pusher" because using, buying, or selling dope is against the law. That doesn't stop some people from using dope. They say they do it to change the way they feel. Often, that means they are trying to run away from their problems. But when the dope wears off, the problems are still there—and they are often worse than before.

There are three drugs we see so often that we sometimes forget they really are drugs. These are alcohol, nicotine, and caffeine. Alcohol is in beer, wine, and liquor. Nicotine is found in cigarettes, cigars, pipe tobacco, and other tobacco products. Caffeine is in coffee, tea, soft drinks, and chocolate. These three drugs are legal. They are sold in stores. But that doesn't mean they are always safe to use. Alcohol and nicotine are such strong drugs that only adults are allowed to buy and use them. And most parents try to keep their children from having too much caffeine.

Marijuana, cocaine, alcohol, nicotine, caffeine, medicines: these are all drugs. All drugs are alike because they change the way our bodies and minds work. But different drugs cause different changes. Some help, and some harm. And when they aren't used properly, even helpful drugs can harm us.

Figuring all this out is not easy. That's why The Drug-Alert Books were written: so you will know why certain drugs are used, how they affect people, why they are dangerous, and what laws there are to control them.

Knowing about drugs is important. It is important to you and to all the people who care about you.

David Friedman, Ph.D.
Consulting Editor

Dr. David Friedman is Deputy Director of the Division of Preclinical Research at the National Institute on Drug Abuse.

The Marijuana Problem

"I knew marijuana messed people up.
But I didn't think it would happen to me."

A real kid said this: a kid with a marijuana problem. He lives in a neighborhood like your neighborhood. He goes to a school like your school.

Marijuana messed up his life. Could it mess up yours?

"Not me," you might say. "I'm too young. I've never even seen the stuff!"

It may surprise you to know that there are kids as young as you who use marijuana. And did you know that one in four teenagers uses marijuana? These are kids in big cities and small towns, in rich neighborhoods and poor ones—and every place in between.

They might even be kids you know.

In fact, there is a good chance that, one day, someone will offer you marijuana.

This is a problem.

It's a problem because marijuana is a very harmful drug. It changes the way people who use it think, feel, and behave. And it is especially harmful to young people.

Marijuana harms the growing bodies of young people. It damages brain cells. It causes lung disease. Marijuana smoke is also known to cause cancer.

Marijuana harms the growing minds of young people. It keeps them from learning about themselves and their world.

It's a problem because marijuana can harm other people, too. It harms our families and friends. It harms people we don't even know.

It's a problem because using marijuana is against the law. People who use or sell it can be arrested and punished, even if they are children.

It's a problem because marijuana is a gateway drug. That means it opens the door to drug problems. Young people who use marijuana are likely to use other illegal drugs, too.

We now know a great deal about the marijuana problem. We know that marijuana is dangerous.

What will you do if someone asks you to use marijuana? It is easier to solve problems if you have the facts. That's why this book was written: to give you the facts you need to know about marijuana.

You will learn why people decide to use marijuana. You will learn how marijuana came to be used in North America and why it is a serious problem today. You will find out what the drug does to the bodies and minds of people who use it. You will find out how it harms everyone, even those who never use it.

But, most important, you will learn how to make the right decision if someone offers you the drug.

Marijuana is a problem. But if you know these things, you will know how to keep it from becoming *your* problem.

Using Marijuana: Why?

Marijuana is a drug with many names.

It wasn't too long ago that "pot" had one meaning: something you cook in. It used to be that "grass" was something you had to mow in the summer. And "tea" was only a drink. But today these words also mean something else: marijuana.

Marijuana comes from a plant called *Cannabis sativa*. (Another name for the cannabis plant is hemp.) Marijuana growers first pick off the leaves and flowering tops of the plant. These are dried and shredded to form a leafy green or brown mixture. This is what we usually call marijuana. It looks like the oregano in your family's herb or spice rack.

Oregano adds a dash of flavor to spaghetti sauce and pizza. That's all it does. But marijuana is a drug: it changes the way people think, feel, and behave.

Many people who use marijuana smoke it in handmade cigarettes called joints. Or they smoke it in pipes. Some people cook with marijuana or drink it, brewed in a marijuana tea.

But no matter *how* they use it, the *reason* they use it is the same: because they want to feel different. A special chemical in the marijuana is what makes people feel different. Its real name is delta-9 tetrahydrocannabinol, but it's called THC for short (**t** for "tetra," **h** for "hydro," and **c** for "cannabinol"). The THC in marijuana makes people feel "high" or "stoned" by changing the way the brain normally works.

Why do people want to use marijuana? And what are the facts about marijuana? Here is what real kids have said about using marijuana and some facts to think about:

> *"It made me feel like I had a lot of friends."*
> Emily (age 13)

FACT: All kids want to have friends. They want to be liked by their peers. A peer is someone who is about the same age as you, someone who does the kinds of things you do. When you feel that other kids are pushing you to do something, you feel peer pressure. Peer pressure is a major reason why many kids smoke their first marijuana cigarette.

Sometimes kids make their own peer pressure. They push themselves to do something because they think "everyone else is doing it." But when it comes to smoking marijuana, everyone else is *not* doing it. Over 15 million kids in junior high and high school do not use marijuana.

That's a lot of peers not smoking marijuana!

> *"I liked the way it made me feel older."*
>
> Marcia (age 13)

FACT: Marijuana may make some kids feel grown up, but that's only because they don't really know what it means to be grown up. In fact, marijuana won't help them grow up any faster. It can actually slow them down.

Growing up is a difficult time for lots of kids. They have to face so many different changes. But when kids use marijuana, they run away from life. Learning how to face the future—without drugs is what *really* helps kids grow up.

One smoker said it best. He first started using marijuana in elementary school. He didn't stop until he was in his twenties. "I'm just starting to learn things I should have learned when I was nine or ten," he said.

> *"If you have a lot of problems, you forget them."*
>
> Jeffrey (age 12)

FACT: Marijuana does not help people forget their problems. When they stop feeling high, they find that their problems have not gone away. If we don't work to solve our problems, they may get worse. And they *will* get worse if people use marijuana to avoid them. Also, people who smoke marijuana are now using an illegal and dangerous drug—and that is always a problem.

> *"It was fun. I laughed a lot."*
>
> Billy (age 14)

FACT: People use marijuana to get high, but often they feel very low instead. They may get scared or feel confused. There is no way to tell how people will feel when they use marijuana. The drug affects different people in different ways. It can even affect the same person in different ways at different times. The fact is that using marijuana changes the way the brain works—and that is always dangerous.

16

A Drug with Many Names

There are nearly 200 names for marijuana. You may have heard it called "pot," "grass," and "weed." But have you heard these?

Airplane	Broccoli	Crying weed
Dry high	Flower	Grasshopper
Hay	Kick stick	Reefer
Salt and pepper	Tea	Wheat

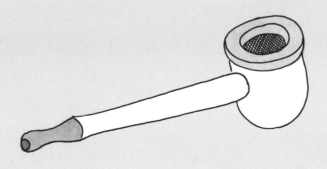

Pot Quiz

People have many different ideas about marijuana. Some are true, some are false. How much do you know? Below are seven statements about marijuana. Do you know if they are true or false?

Answer true or false to these statements. Then, see how much you know about marijuana by looking at the answers on the next page. You will find out more about marijuana as you read the chapters to come.

1. Marijuana is a new drug.

2. Marijuana is less harmful to the lungs than tobacco.

3. Most marijuana users get their first joint from a stranger.

4. Most kids use marijuana at least once.

5. Kids are too young to get arrested for using marijuana.

6. It's safe to use marijuana and drive a car.

7. It's hard to say "No" when a friend offers you marijuana.

Let's see how you did.

1. **False.** Marijuana is one of the oldest drugs in the world—over 5,000 years old. (See Chapter 3.)

2. **False.** Marijuana can be even more harmful to the lungs than tobacco. (See Chapter 4.)

3. **False.** Most users get their first joint from a friend. (See Chapter 4.)

4. **False.** Most kids never use marijuana. (See Chapter 6.)

5. **False.** Kids can be arrested and punished for using marijuana no matter how young they are. (See Chapter 5.)

6. **False.** Using marijuana is a cause of many accidents. (See Chapter 5.)

7. **True.** Saying "No" to marijuana may not be easy. But it can be done. Most kids do say "No" to marijuana and other drugs. (See Chapter 6.)

Marijuana: A History

The marijuana plant has been grown for over 5,000 years and has been used in many different ways. The ancient Chinese used the fibers of the marijuana plant to weave rope and clothing. The Greeks and Romans made medicines from marijuana. Other people pressed the cannabis seeds to make oil for soap and paint. The seeds of the cannabis plant were even used for birdseed.

3000 B.C.   500 B.C.   50 B.C.

But there was one other use for the marijuana plant. Since the earliest times, people have used marijuana to get high.

Like the people of ancient China or Rome, the American colonists grew and used the marijuana plant. In the 1600s and 1700s, they used hemp fibers to make rope for their tall sailing ships. Many of their clothes were also woven from hemp. In the 1800s, when American settlers moved to the Western frontier, the canvas tops of their covered wagons were sometimes made from the fibers of the marijuana plant.

Unlike people in other countries, Americans did not use marijuana to get high until the 1900s. Marijuana was a legal drug then, as alcohol is today. Using marijuana to get stoned became popular in the United States during the 1920s and 1930s. As more people began to smoke marijuana, others began to believe that it was very dangerous, especially to

1600s   1800s   1900s

21

young people. Government officials called marijuana a "public health menace." Newspaper stories showed marijuana as "The Assassin of Youth." School teachers, youth club sponsors, and church leaders all warned young people to stay away from marijuana. The "health menace" of marijuana was also seen in popular magazines and movies. One movie made in 1936, *Reefer Madness*, described marijuana as "the public enemy number one."

In those years, there was a real concern about the health dangers of marijuana. But some of what was said and written about marijuana was not true. In the movie *Reefer Madness*, for example, people become violent or crazy after just one puff of marijuana. That just does not happen in real life. These stories about marijuana were supposed to scare people away

1920s   1930s

from the drug—and that's what they did. Many people were afraid of marijuana, and laws were passed to control its use. In America, from 1914 to 1931, 29 states made using marijuana illegal. Then, in 1937, the Marijuana Tax Act, a law passed by the United States Congress, restricted the use of marijuana everywhere in the United States.

Some of these laws made the sale or use of marijuana a misdemeanor. A misdemeanor is not the most serious kind of crime. People are usually given a fine or go to jail for a short time if they are found guilty of a misdemeanor. In later years, new and tougher laws were passed against "the public enemy number one." Marijuana use became a felony. A felony is a very serious crime, like robbery or murder. People usually go to jail for a long time if they are found guilty of a felony.

MISDEMEANOR

FELONY

1940s   1950s

Even though marijuana was illegal, some people kept on using it. In the 1960s, marijuana became more popular than ever. College and even high school students began using the drug. To many young people, using marijuana was a way to show how mature and independent they were. They wanted to lead their own lives in their own way. The "hippies" and "flower children" of the 1960s made marijuana a part of their way of life.

But marijuana wasn't just used by hippies and students. Many people were smoking pot in the 1960s and 1970s. They did not believe that it was really dangerous. They remembered the old stories of people "losing their minds" after smoking marijuana. That didn't happen to them. Not all doctors and scientists thought marijuana was harmful either. They were

1960s   1970s

just beginning to learn about the drug, so they did not know as much about it as we do today. And marijuana *seemed* safe when compared with other drugs.

As marijuana was used more and more, there were many people who started to think that the punishment for smoking pot was too harsh. Most of the states changed their laws once more, and marijuana use became a misdemeanor again.

In the 1970s and 1980s, more studies on marijuana use showed scientists that it is, in fact, a very harmful drug. Now, the news about pot is getting out to more and more people. Today, fewer people are using marijuana, and fewer young people ever try marijuana at all. That's the good news. But the bad news is that marijuana is still the most widely used illegal drug.

1980s

Getting the Marijuana Message

According to a recent survey, "our attitudes about marijuana use are changing." People, especially young people, are beginning to get the message that marijuana is a dangerous drug. What did the survey find?

- Fewer people are using marijuana. In 1985, 18 million people used marijuana. In 1988, that number was down to 12 million.

- Fewer young people are using marijuana. In 1985, 5.8 percent of 12 and 13 year olds used marijuana. In 1988, that number was down to 4.2 percent.

- More young people are aware of the dangers of using marijuana. In 1985, 37 percent of young people thought smoking marijuana was a "great risk." In 1988, that number increased to 44 percent.

But marijuana use is still a major drug problem. Millions of young people continue to use marijuana. It remains the most widely used illegal drug.

There are over 65 million people in the United States and Canada who have used marijuana. Over 11 million people use it at least once a month. Almost one-half of all high school students have used it. And many younger people, some as young as you, have used it, too.

Today, marijuana is a special problem because:

- Very young kids are using marijuana. Drugs like marijuana are now found in junior high and even elementary schools.

- Marijuana is stronger than ever before. Marijuana growers have found ways to make the drug much stronger than it was in the 1960s.

- Buying and selling drugs is a dangerous—and sometimes deadly—business.

There is more to learn about marijuana. We don't know all of the facts yet. Even so, we already know a good deal about what marijuana does to the body and mind. And we *know* that using marijuana is dangerous.

What happens to someone who smokes marijuana?

Let's meet Mark.

What Does Marijuana Do?

Mark is an imaginary boy. But he is not much different from other boys and girls.

Mark is 13 years old. He enjoys school, at least most of the time. He plays baseball after school. On the weekend, he likes to skateboard with his friends. And he also loves to read adventure stories. When he's riding his bike, Mark pretends he's on an adventure of his own.

Like other boys and girls his age, Mark has plans for his future. He dreams about becoming a jet pilot.

There's one other thing about Mark you should know: he smokes marijuana.

Like most other kids who smoke marijuana, Mark was asked to use pot for the first time by his friends. The first time they asked him to use it, he said "No." And he said "No" the second time they asked him, and the third time, too. Saying "No" was hard for Mark. He didn't like being the only one who wasn't smoking marijuana. "Why shouldn't I join my friends?" he asked himself. "It doesn't seem to hurt them."

It took Mark's friends a few days to talk him into sharing a joint with them. But, finally, he used it. He didn't like it much the first time he smoked it. It burned his throat and made him feel dizzy. But Mark's friends kept asking him to use it again. A week later, he smoked pot again. Now, Mark smokes marijuana two or three times a week.

Mark knows that marijuana changes the way he feels. He knows it makes him feel lightheaded. He knows that it makes his mouth dry and his eyes red. He can feel his heart beat faster when he smokes marijuana.

But smoking marijuana changes Mark in other ways, too. It changes him in ways he doesn't even know about.

Mark needs oxygen to live. His body gets new oxygen every time he breathes. But when Mark smokes marijuana, his body breathes in lots of harmful chemicals, too, including THC. The marijuana smoke goes down Mark's nose and throat and through his trachea (or windpipe). The trachea looks like an upside-down tree trunk. In fact, it has two upside-down branches called bronchial tubes. One branch goes to the right lung, and one goes to the left lung. The marijuana smoke flows through the bronchial tubes and into the lungs. There, the harmful chemicals enter Mark's bloodstream. It takes only 6 or 7 seconds for his heart to pump the THC to every part of his body. In about 10 minutes, Mark begins to feel different. The THC in marijuana is changing the way his brain works.

The brain helps us do many things:

• Senses

The brain receives information from our senses. We can see, hear, touch, taste, and smell the world around us because the brain receives signals from our eyes, ears, skin, tongue, and nose.

• Movement

The brain tells our bodies to move. We can walk and run, skip and dance, reach up and down, snap our fingers, and move our lips because the brain tells our muscles when and how to move.

• Thoughts

The brain does our thinking. We can plan for the future, remember the past, figure things out, solve problems, and make decisions because we use our brains to think and learn.

• Feelings

The brain gives us our feelings. We can be happy or sad, hopeful or afraid, relaxed or angry because the brain makes us feel that way.

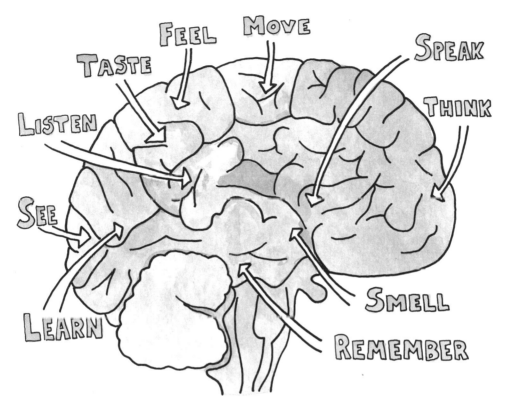

But when Mark is high, he may have trouble doing these things. His brain may not be able to use the information he gets from his senses. He may not be able to control the way his body moves. He may not be able to make good decisions. Marijuana keeps the brain from doing the job it's supposed to do in the way it's supposed to do it.

31

If Mark plays baseball after he smokes marijuana, he may think he's playing really well. But his teammates know he's not. Mark may not be able to follow the ball well enough with his eyes. He may have a slower reaction time: that means it will take him too long to swing the bat or raise his glove to catch the ball. He may not be on the team for long.

It could also be dangerous for Mark to ride his bike or his skateboard after he has smoked marijuana. The doctors and nurses who work in hospital emergency rooms know that marijuana and good coordination don't go together. They see many people who hurt themselves when they are high.

Mark has trouble paying attention when he's high. Have you ever felt so tired at school that it was hard to keep your mind on your work? If the teacher called on you, you probably didn't understand the question. Or maybe you forgot—in just a few seconds—what the question was. That's how Mark's mind works when he smokes marijuana.

Imagine trying to have an important conversation with someone whose mind works like that! Mark may have trouble completing his thoughts, or he may wander from one idea to another. And, sometimes, the things he says just don't make any sense.

Time seems to slow down for Mark when he is high. If he listens to the radio for only a few minutes, he might think one or two hours have passed. The clock doesn't change when Mark smokes pot, but his brain does.

Mark's brain changes in other ways, too. As you read this book, your brain is helping you to learn. Later on, you will remember some of the things you are reading right now. But if Mark reads when he is high, he might not remember anything, even though he loves to read. That's because marijuana makes it harder to remember new things, even things that only happened a short time ago.

When Mark uses marijuana, his moods may change, too. Sometimes, pot gives Mark a lightheaded kind of feeling: "Sort of like I'm floating," he says. But, other times, using marijuana may make Mark feel nervous or anxious. "I know I should be studying," he might think. Or he might worry, "If my parents ever catch me, they'll ground me forever." Mark may feel too worried about everyday things. Or he may get suspicious of other people. "Why are they talking about me?" he may ask himself, when no one is talking about him at all.

Mark could have even more frightening experiences. Some people have panic reactions when they use marijuana. They may feel completely out of control and terrified of the world around them.

Mark may feel the effects of marijuana anywhere from five minutes to three hours. It depends on how strong the marijuana is and how much of it Mark smokes. When the marijuana wears off, Mark starts to feel tired and sad. He gets a "worn out kind of feeling." This feeling is called a marijuana hangover. You probably know what happens to people who drink too much. They feel sick when the alcohol wears off.

Mark will not have that kind of hangover, but, like many marijuana users, his mood or spirit may change. When the marijuana wears off, Mark is likely to feel very low.

A few hours later, Mark's marijuana hangover is gone. He feels better. But the marijuana hasn't left his body yet.

Most of the foods we eat stay in our bodies for a few days. What we drink passes out of the body in only a few hours. But THC remains in the body for a long time. The THC from just one joint can stay in the body for more than a week. If someone smokes marijuana several times in one week, it may take up to a month for all the THC to leave the body.

THC stays in the body's fatty tissues. Even the thinnest people have lots of fatty tissues inside them. The kidneys, lungs, and reproductive organs are especially fatty. So is the brain. THC stays in these parts of the body and returns little by little into the bloodstream.

This means that if he smokes several joints every week, Mark always has some THC in his body—whether he feels it or not. And the THC is hurting Mark—whether he knows it or not.

The longer Mark uses marijuana, the more damage it can do. Like every 13 year old, Mark has a lot of growing, and a lot of growing up, to do. But if he keeps on smoking pot, it may be hard for Mark to become a healthy adult.

Marijuana will hurt Mark's body. Smoking pot is even more likely to cause cancer and hurt the lungs than smoking cigarettes. The cells of the brain and the nervous system are also damaged by marijuana. And marijuana destroys the body's white blood cells. These cells fight infections and diseases, so marijuana users may get sick more than other people.

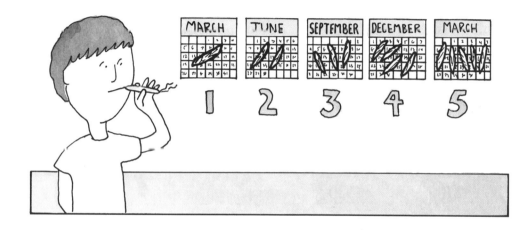

The more Mark smokes, the harder it will be for him to stop. He might develop a tolerance to marijuana. This means he will get used to the drug and need more and more of it to get high. He might develop a dependence on marijuana. This means he will *need* to smoke pot to feel normal. Without marijuana, he will feel moody and depressed. This sick feeling is called marijuana withdrawal.

Mark smoked his first joint about six months ago. Now, he wants to smoke marijuana as much as he likes to play baseball, read adventure books, and ride his bike. Soon, he may want to smoke it even more. He may feel that marijuana is more important than school, sports, and his hobbies—more important than anything else. This problem develops in young people who use a lot of marijuana (or any other drug) over a long period of time. It is called amotivational syndrome.

That's a difficult name, but it's a simple idea: young people who have this problem lose interest in just about everything but smoking pot. They no longer care about how they look. They no longer care about eating well or being in good shape. They no longer care about school. They no longer care about their friends or families. They no longer care about the future. Their lives are a mess—and they don't even care.

If he keeps on smoking marijuana, Mark may stop dreaming about becoming a jet pilot. He may stop planning for his future. He may stop wanting to be or do anything at all.

Mark is an imaginary boy. But there is nothing "made up" about what marijuana does to his body and mind. It is a real problem. It is happening to real kids today. Each year, over 70,000 young people enter drug abuse programs because of their marijuana problems. Here is what some of them have to say:

"School used to be an okay place, but when I started getting high a lot, I hated it."

Ted (age 15)

"My Mom used to help me shop for really nice clothes. But none of the druggies I hung out with dressed like that. I just didn't care how I looked."

Michele (age 16)

"I have a great telescope. I used to look through it whenever there was a clear night. I would keep charts and records. I thought about studying astronomy in college. When I got heavy into pot, though, I hardly touched it. I'm just beginning to get interested in it again."

Patty (age 15)

Marijuana and Health

In the last 20 years, scientists have learned that marijuana is much more dangerous than people used to think. Here are some of the health problems caused by marijuana:

- Marijuana smoke contains poisonous gases and chemicals. Like the gases and chemicals in cigarette smoke, these poisons are known to cause cancer.

- Marijuana smoke can destroy lung tissue. It makes it harder to breathe and causes diseases of the lungs.

- Marijuana hurts the immune system. Smoking pot may make it easier for people to get sick.

- Marijuana changes the way the brain works. Smoking pot makes it hard to think clearly and remember things.

- If pregnant women smoke marijuana, the drug will hurt their unborn babies.

Marijuana and Our World

Suppose a person who uses marijuana tells you, "So what if I smoke pot? I'm not hurting anyone but myself." Is that right? Do you agree? What would you say?

Marijuana users do hurt other people: people they know and even people they don't know.

Marijuana smokers hurt their families and friends. This is how one father felt when his son had a marijuana problem:

"It was hard to watch someone you love destroy himself and pull others down with him."

Smoking marijuana hurts other people, too. You already know how dangerous it is to drink and drive. But did you know that it is just as dangerous to use pot and drive?

Using marijuana causes many other kinds of accidents, too. In fact, over one-third of all accident victims have been found to have marijuana in their blood. This is not surprising when you remember what marijuana does to the people who use it:

- They may not see things well.
- They have trouble paying attention.
- They usually don't react to things quickly.

Smoking marijuana is illegal. People who grow, sell, buy, or use marijuana—no matter how young they are—are breaking the law. They are also involved with other people who break the law. And that can be dangerous, too.

The people who sell marijuana are called "dealers" or "pushers." Dealers sell marijuana and other drugs to make money, not to make friends. They may be part of drug gangs. Gang members usually carry guns—and they are not afraid to use them. One police officer who works with young people says, "Wherever you find drugs, you'll find guns, too." The world of drugs is a very dangerous one.

Members of organized crime groups bring marijuana into the United States from other countries. This practice is known as smuggling. Smugglers sneak marijuana into the country in many ways. They stuff it into backpacks or hide it in false bottoms of suitcases. It is hidden in cars and trucks. It is secretly flown in on airplanes and shipped in on boats.

42

Marijuana, Kids, and the Law

It is against the law everywhere for kids to have, use, buy, or sell any amount of marijuana. Kids who do may find themselves in trouble—big trouble—no matter how young they are. This is what happened to one girl who brought marijuana to school:

- A teacher thought he saw her smoking marijuana and searched her belongings.

- The teacher found marijuana in her locker.

- The teacher took her to the principal.

- The principal called the police.

- The police arrested her and took her to the police station.

- The police questioned and fingerprinted her.

- The police called her parents to take her home.

- She had to go to juvenile court, a special court for young people.

- The judge at juvenile court made her go to a drug counseling program.

- The principal suspended her from school.

Officials of the United States government try to stop drugs from coming into the country. Their job is to check people who are entering the country to make sure they are not carrying drugs. They also try to catch people who sneak into the country with drugs. But it is a very difficult job to do because:

- So many people—over 300 million—and vehicles enter the United States every year.

- America is such a big country. There are thousands and thousands of miles of coastline where drug smugglers can enter without being seen.

- Smugglers bring marijuana into the country in so many ways. One search team found 26 tons of marijuana on a foreign fishing boat. It was hidden under 40 tons of frozen sharks. In California, an oil tanker truck from Mexico was loaded with over 50 gallons of oil—and 1,100 pounds of marijuana.

- There aren't enough government workers to stop the drug smuggling. Drug enforcement officials say that they find only 10% of all the illegal drugs people smuggle into the United States.

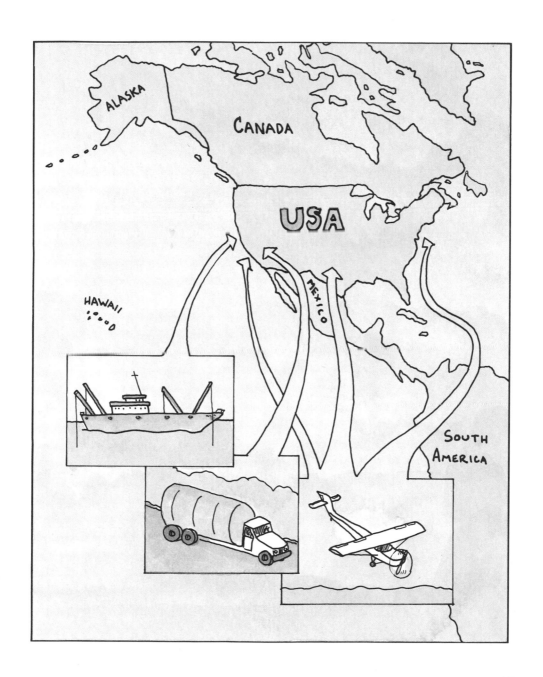

Smuggling isn't the only way marijuana gets into the United States. Lots of marijuana is grown in the United States. People grow it on their own land. And they grow it on land that belongs to all of us, too.

Have you ever heard the song that goes: "This land is your land, this land is my land"? America's 156 national forests are for everyone to enjoy. They have shady trails to hike on, cool lakes to swim in, and high mountains to climb. These forests are also a home for many wild animals.

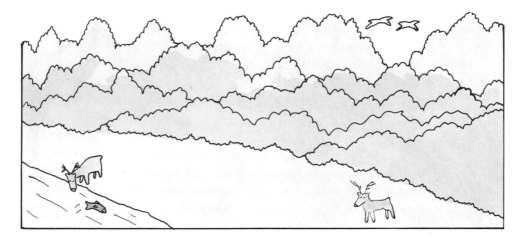

But marijuana growers want this land to be *their* land. They have taken over certain parts of the national forests to plant and grow marijuana. They protect the crop with fierce dogs, dangerous booby traps, and guns. The United States Forest Service has had to close off many parts of our land to keep people from getting hurt by marijuana growers.

And people aren't the only victims. One Forest Service official says he knows that marijuana is nearby when he begins to see dead animals in the area.

Sometimes, marijuana growers spread poisons around their plants to keep rats and squirrels from eating them. The poisons kill these animals and also the larger animals, like foxes, that eat rats and squirrels. The fertilizers used to grow marijuana are poisonous to animals, too. These poisons and

chemicals also wash into the streams, where they injure or kill the animals that live in the water or come to drink it. And, sometimes, pot growers try to protect their crops by shooting the animals, like deer, that eat the young and tender shoots of marijuana plants.

So, if a marijuana smoker tells you, "I'm only hurting myself," you know what to say. It just isn't true.

The Tale of Cowboy: Detector Dog

Cowboy is a black Labrador retriever. He was one year old when he was adopted from an animal shelter in Georgia and taken to a training center in Virginia. There, he learned to find drugs by using his good sense of smell. Cowboy started a new life as a detector dog.

Over 160 dogs help the United States government find drugs that people try to smuggle into the country. All kinds of dogs are used for this job, but mostly retrievers like Cowboy. That's because retrievers love to chase and find things. It is Cowboy's special job to find marijuana. He works at the Port of Miami in Florida with his partner, a man named Lee Titus.

Since 1970, the U.S. Customs Service has used these detector dogs to check airplanes, cars, trucks, and boats for drugs. In 1984, a search team brought a detector dog onto a freight ship. The dog sniffed at a large pile of gravel. Then, he scratched it with his paw: that meant he smelled drugs. The search team used two small bulldozers to clear away the gravel, which was six feet deep. Underneath it all were 36 tons of marijuana!

Lee had to train Cowboy to be a detector dog. He would roll up a towel covered with the smell of marijuana and throw it as far as he could. Then, Cowboy would run to the towel, pick it up with his teeth, and run back to Lee. Cowboy and Lee would play a game of tug-of-war with the towel. And Lee would always let Cowboy win.

When Cowboy got good at that game, Lee would roll real marijuana into the towel. After a while, Cowboy knew that if he found the hidden marijuana, he could play a friendly game of tug-of-war with Lee.

Now, whenever Cowboy finds marijuana at the Port of Miami, Lee gives him a special suitcase. Cowboy plays with the suitcase until he finds the rolled-up towel Lee put inside. Then, it's tug-of-war time for Cowboy and Lee.

Marijuana and You

What if someone asked you to smoke marijuana? Do you know what you would do?

You've heard that you should "Just Say No" to drugs. That's because saying "No" to drugs means saying "Yes" to:

- your good health

- your family and friends

- feeling good about yourself

- setting a good example for other kids

- drug-free schools and neighborhoods

- safe roads

- your future

Saying "No" sounds like it should be easy. After all, "No" is probably one of the first words you learned when you were a baby! You said it then because you wanted to do things by yourself.

Now, as you're on your way to becoming an adult, you still want to do things in your own way. The difference is that you also want to do what your friends are doing. And if your friends are smoking marijuana and asking you to join them, saying "No" can be pretty hard.

But think about this: more and more young people are saying "No" to pot all the time. Over 15 million young people have never tried marijuana. Many say their friends wouldn't like them to smoke marijuana. Now, that's the kind of peer pressure that can help kids say "No"! They also know that using marijuana is a way of hurting themselves and the world around them.

But even if you know all these things, it may still be hard to say "No." Now, you know *why* to say "No" to marijuana. But you also need to know *how* to say "No."

There are lots of ways to say "No." Here are some you can use. Choose the ones that work best for you, or think of your own. Practice them in front of a mirror or with a friend. Be ready to "Just Say No."

Ten Ways to Say "No"

1. No thanks, I'm allergic.
2. I'm not in the mood.
3. I'm taking medicine, and I can't mix it with other drugs.
4. I can't. I have lots of homework, and I want to think straight.
5. No. I'm going to ride my bike. Want to come?
6. It burns my throat.
7. No way. It's against the law.
8. My parents would kill me. Wouldn't yours?
9. No. It's bad for your lungs, and I need my lungs for baseball.
10. Nope. I don't want to kill my brain cells!

And you can also help other kids. When *Weekly Reader* magazine asked 4th, 5th, and 6th graders how kids can help other kids stay away from drugs, this is what they said:

- "Teach younger kids about the dangers."

- "Encourage other kids to say 'No.'"

- "Report drug sellers to parents or the principal."

- "Encourage kids who use drugs to seek help."

- "Learn the facts about drugs."

You have learned the facts about marijuana from reading this book. You know that marijuana is a problem, especially for young people. You know that marijuana is a problem you may one day have to face.

You also know what to do and what to say if someone offers you marijuana. You know the right decision. You know how to say "No."

Now, you know how to keep the marijuana problem from becoming *your* problem.

Glossary

amotivational syndrome	the feeling that nothing in life is worth doing
cannabis	the plant from which marijuana comes; *Cannabis sativa*
dealer	a person who sells illegal drugs; another word for pusher
dependence	the way the body and brain need a drug to avoid feeling sick
drug	a substance that changes the way the brain works
felony	a crime (such as murder or burglary) that is more serious than a misdemeanor
gateway drug	a drug that can lead to other drug problems
hangover	the sick feeling that people get after drug use
hemp	another word for the marijuana (or cannabis) plant
high	a term used to describe the effects of marijuana

joint	a marijuana cigarette
marijuana	a drug that comes from the cannabis (or hemp) plant
misdemeanor	a crime that is less serious than a felony
panic reaction	a feeling of great fear and loss of control
peer pressure	the feeling that you have to do what other people your age are doing
pot	another name for marijuana
pusher	another word for dealer
reefer	another name for marijuana or a marijuana cigarette
smuggling	sneaking illegal drugs into a country
stoned	another word for high
THC	the chemical in the marijuana plant that changes the way the brain works; *delta-9 tetrahydrocannabinol*
tolerance	the way the body and brain need more and more of a drug to get the same effect
withdrawal	the sick feeling drug users get when they can't get the drugs they are dependent on

Index